British Insects and Other Minibeasts

Clare Collinson

W
FRANKLIN WATTS
LONDON·SYDNEY

Franklin Watts
First published in Great Britain in paperback in 2018 by The Watts
Publishing Group.

Copyright © The Watts Publishing Group 2016

All rights reserved.

Planning and production by Discovery Books Limited
Managing Editor: Laura Durman
Editor: Clare Collinson
Design: sprout.uk.com
Picture research: Clare Collinson

ISBN: 978 1 4451 3633 2

Printed in China

Franklin Watts
An imprint of
Hachette Children's Group
Part of The Watts Publishing Group
Carmelite House
50 Victoria Embankment
London EC4Y 0DZ

An Hachette UK Company
www.hachette.co.uk
www.franklinwatts.co.uk

FSC
www.fsc.org
MIX
Paper from
responsible sources
FSC® C104740

Picture credits: Alamy: p. 16 (Kim Taylor/Nature Picture Library), p.
19t (macana), p. 27b (Andrew Darrington), p. 29t
(Nigel Cattlin), p. 30r (OJO Images Ltd); Bigstock: p. 6 (Ulio),
p. 27t (Marietjieopp); FLPA: p. 10t (Bert Pijs/Minden Pictures),
p. 13br (Malcolm Schuyl), p. 15b (Derek Middleton), p. 17bl (Peter
Entwistle), p. 22 (Derek Middleton), p. 24 (John Eveson), p. 25b
(Malcolm Schuyl), p. 30l (Angela Hampton); Shutterstock: title
page (Lyudmyla Kharlamova), pp. 3, 31 (Eric Isselee, jps, Marco
Uliana, Dani Vincek), p. 4 (Radka Palenikova), p. 5 (Karel Gallas),
p. 7t (Johan van Beilen), p. 7b (EBFoto), p. 8 (Ian Grainger),
p. 9t (bjonesphotography), p. 9b (schankz), p. 10b (Tomatito),
p. 11t (Quick Shot), p. 11b (N Mrtgh), p. 12 (Philip Bird), p. 13t
(Martin Fowler), p. 13bl (neil hardwick), p. 14 (hakuna_jina),
p. 15t (Torsten Dietrich), p. 17t (Vitalii Hulai), p. 17br (lkpro),
p. 18l (Sue Robinson), p. 18r (Photo Fun), p. 19b (Jaclyn Schreiner),
p. 20t (Nastya22), p. 20b (stevie_uk), p. 21t (Quayside),
p. 21b (Dimijana), p. 23t (Mauro Rodrigues), p. 23b (Henrik
Larsson), p. 25t (Valentyn Volkov), p. 26 (Imfoto), p. 28 (Artush),
p. 29b (scubaluna), p. 31 (holbox), p. 31 (Marco Prati), p. 31
(paulrommer), p. 31 (holbox, Marco Prati, paulrommer, motorolka).

Cover photo: Shutterstock (inkwelldodo).

Every attempt has been made to clear copyright. Should there be any
inadvertent omission please apply to the publisher for rectification.

Useful websites

Amateur Entomologists' Society: Insects
www.amentsoc.org/insects/
Facts about British insects and other invertebrates, including
information about the classification of insect groups.

BugLife – The Invertebrate Conservation Trust
www.buglife.org.uk
Information about the conservation of minibeasts, as
well as activities and identification pages.

Minibeasts in Your Garden
*www.lrwt.org.uk/media/uploads/wildlife/minibeasts_
in_your_garden_ne_leaflet.pdf*
A downloadable booklet full of information about
minibeasts to look for in British gardens.

Natural England
www.naturalengland.org.uk
Find out about conservation projects to protect British
wildlife, including minibeasts such as the field cricket.

The Wildlife Trusts UK
www.wildlifetrusts.org
Discover more about all British wildlife. There is a species
explorer page with information about minibeasts.

Wildlife Watch: Minibeasts
*www.wildlifewatch.org.uk/explore-wildlife/
animals/minibeasts*
Find out how to take part in a 'wildlife watch', hunt for
minibeasts, and take part in other events in your local area.

Woodland Trust Nature Detectives
www.naturedetectives.org.uk/packs/minibeast_pack.htm
Lots of minibeast activities to download and print.

Young People's Trust for the Environment
www.ypte.org.uk/animal/minibeasts/30
Information about minibeasts, including where they
live, what they eat and how they are classified.

*Note to parents and teachers: Every effort has been made
to ensure that these websites contain no inappropriate or
offensive material. However, because of the nature of the
Internet, it is impossible to guarantee that the contents
of these sites will not be altered. We strongly advise that
Internet access is supervised by a responsible adult.*

Contents

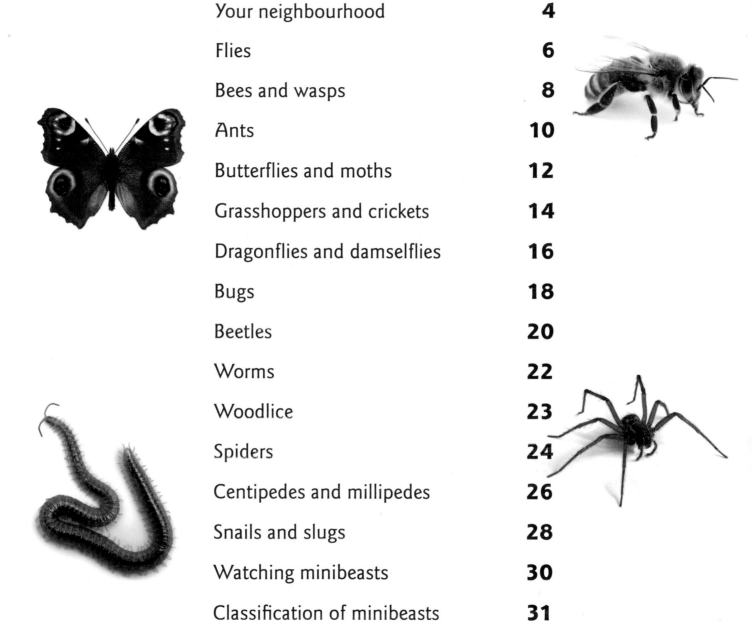

Words that appear in **bold** in the text are explained in the glossary.

Your neighbourhood

There are more insects in British neighbourhoods than any other kind of animal. So wherever you live, you'll find a huge variety of insects nearby. There are also many other minibeasts to discover, such as worms, bugs and snails.

Inside and outside

From spiders that run across our ceilings to woodlice that lurk in our cellars, many minibeasts find a perfect **habitat** in our homes. Once you start looking outside, you'll find a whole miniature world to explore, from beetles and butterflies to centipedes and crickets.

In the summer, you will find butterflies, such as this marbled white, wherever there are lots of flowers.

Minibeast hunting

Insects and other minibeasts live wherever they can find food and shelter. The secret to finding them is to know where to look. Search for them on plants and trees, and in piles of wood. Start rummaging around, lifting up stones and looking through leaves. You will be amazed at how many you find.

When to look

The best time to find insects and other minibeasts is in the spring and summer, when they are most active.

What is a minibeast?

Minibeasts are the little creatures you might call bugs or creepy-crawlies. Scientists call these animals **invertebrates**, which means they do not have backbones. Some minibeasts, such as insects and spiders, have hard casings outside their bodies called exoskeletons.

Beetles are a kind of insect. Of all British beetles, the stag beetle is the largest. It might look a bit scary, but it is completely harmless.

What is an insect?

Insects are a special group of minibeasts that have certain things in common.
- All insects have six legs.
- All insects have a body divided into three parts – the head, **thorax** and **abdomen**.
- Most insects have two pairs of wings.
- Most insects have **antennae**, or feelers.

Minibeast habitats

All minibeasts have their own preferred habitat. You'll find them easier to spot if you know what they like to eat or where they lay their eggs. Baby stag beetles, or **larvae**, feed on rotting wood, so you might find an adult stag beetle like the one below in a pile of logs.

Flies

Of all the insects in your neighbourhood, flies are the ones you'll probably see most often. They are found in all habitats in Britain, from cities to mountain tops. Just open your kitchen window on a summer's day and a fly will come buzzing in.

Unique insects

Some insects, such as dragonflies and damselflies, have the word 'fly' as part of their name. In fact, they are not flies at all. True flies are unique in the insect world. They are the only insects with just one pair of wings.

House guest

As you might guess from its name, the housefly is the fly that's most likely to come into your home, but it's an unwelcome visitor. It can spread disease by landing on your food after feeding on rotting waste or even animal poo!

Orderly group

True flies form a group, or **order**, of insects called diptera, which means 'two wings'. They are the largest order of animals in Britain, with around 7,000 known **species**.

*When houseflies land on our surfaces and food, they leave small bits of dirt and **bacteria** behind.*

Fly in disguise

This harmless hoverfly has a clever disguise. You could easily mistake it for a wasp. Its black and yellow markings trick **predators**, such as birds, into thinking it is dangerous.

Liquid diet

It might seem surprising, but flies do not eat solid food. Instead, they have special sponge-like **mouthparts** for sucking up liquid. Some flies feed on rotting fruit or sweet **nectar** from flowers. Others, such as female mosquitoes, will only suck blood.

From egg to adult

Like all insects, a fly changes its appearance at different stages of its life. Female flies lay eggs that hatch into wingless larvae called maggots. The larvae feed and grow before changing into **pupae**. Then the adult flies emerge and fly away. This process is called metamorphosis.

The hoverfly feeds on nectar from flowers.

Daddy-long-legs

With its long, thin legs, the daddy-long-legs, or crane fly, is easy to recognise. These gangly flies sometimes appear in great numbers in September, when the adults hatch from the pupae.

Adult crane flies only live for a week or two.

Bees and wasps

In summer, our gardens and parks hum with busy bees. You're sure to have seen them buzzing from flower to flower. And you've probably been bothered by wasps, as they try to join in your picnic or even taste your ice cream!

British bees

There are about 250 species of bee in Britain, but the most familiar are the honeybee and the bumblebee. You'll recognise bumblebees by their big, furry bodies. Honeybees are smaller and they have less fur.

There are 24 species of bumblebee in Britain. Each species has different markings, but they all have bodies covered in dense fur.

Living together

Many bees live alone, but bumblebees and honeybees live in groups called colonies. Bumblebees live in nests, which usually house a colony of around 200 bees. A honeybee colony is much larger, often containing as many as 60,000 bees. Most honeybees live in hives kept by beekeepers.

Busy as a bee

The honeybees and bumblebees that you see on flowers are female worker bees gathering nectar and **pollen**. Back in the nest or hive, the workers also make honey, feed the **queen bee** and take care of all the young bees.

Pollen basket

Honeybees pack pollen into special 'pollen baskets' on their back legs. When the baskets are full, they take the pollen back to the hive.

Perfect pollinators

You may have honey on your toast for breakfast, but you probably have bees to thank for your lunch and tea, too. By carrying pollen from one flower to another, bees **pollinate** flowers. This makes the plants produce fruit and seeds. Without bees, many of the fruits and vegetables we eat would not grow.

Wasp homes

Have you ever come across a wasps' nest? Wasps are expert nest-builders. They make papery homes in holes in the ground, trees, garden sheds and even in people's lofts.

A taste for sugar

Have you ever wondered why wasps seem to love sweet, fizzy drinks? Adult wasps feed on nectar and a sugary liquid produced by their larvae. Towards the end of summer, this food begins to run out. That's when wasps start looking elsewhere!

Wasp or bee?

Wasps look similar to bees, but they have less fur on their bodies. Wasps are more aggressive, and are more likely to sting you if they get annoyed.

If you see a wasps' nest, keep away!

Ants

In summer, you'll easily find ants in your neighbourhood. Most ants live in nests outside but you might see them scurry into your kitchen, searching for sugary treats.

Black and red...
The ants you're most likely to see are black garden ants. They often make nests under pavements and paving slabs, and close to walls. You'll see red ants in piles of rotting wood and under stones.

...and yellow
If you see small mounds of soil on a garden lawn or in a field, you'll know yellow meadow ants are nesting below. You might mistake these ants for red ants because of their orangey-yellow colour, but these ants won't sting you.

Up close

Black garden ants are harmless to humans – they will not sting or bite you. If you want to look at an ant close up, let a black garden ant crawl on to your hand and look at it through a magnifying glass.

Don't try to catch red ants (below) – they can give you a painful sting.

Yellow meadow ants (above) are not often seen above ground unless their nest is disturbed.

Nesting skills

Ants are among the most skilled nest-builders of all insects found in Britain. Below ground, they make a huge network of underground tunnels and chambers where thousands of ants live and breed.

Working together

Like some bees and wasps, ants live in large, organised colonies. Most of the ants you'll see are female workers searching for food. Working together, they often attack **prey** much bigger than themselves.

When ants find food, they leave a scent trail for other ants to follow.

A home in the forest

The nests that wood ants create are among the most impressive of all nests you'll see. They make large, cone-shaped nests in pine forests, using pine needles, twigs and leaves.

Large wood ants' nests like this one often house about 100,000 ants.

Ant attack!

If you see a wood ants' nest, don't touch it. When wood ants sense danger, they squirt out a smelly liquid to scare off predators. This is usually not harmful to humans, but could sting if it gets into your eye.

Butterflies and moths

On warm days in spring and summer, our gardens, parks and meadows come alive with delicate butterflies. You'll see them fluttering from flower to flower. After the sun has gone down, take a torch outside and moths will be drawn to the light.

Spectacular wings

Butterflies and moths have the largest wings in the insect world. Each species has its own pattern. And there are lots of different colours to spot, from white, blue and yellow to orange, red and copper.

Eye-catching

One of the most stunning butterflies you'll see is the peacock butterfly. It has four eye-like markings on its wings, which look a bit like the pattern on a peacock's feathers.

The eyespots on a peacock butterfly's wings help to scare off hungry predators.

British moths and butterflies

There are over 2,500 types of moth in Britain, but fewer than 70 species of butterfly.

Moth or butterfly?

An easy way to tell butterflies and moths apart is to watch them while they are still. Butterflies usually rest with their wings together, while moths hold their wings flat.

Spot the moth

Most moths are less colourful than butterflies but their markings can be just as beautiful. During the day, they are good at keeping out of sight, so it might be hard to find them.

Hungry caterpillars

Butterflies and moths begin their lives as eggs, which hatch into hungry larvae called caterpillars. Many caterpillars are green, so they are hard to spot against the leaves and plants they feed on. Others are brightly coloured to scare off predators and some are covered in fuzzy hairs.

*Many moths, such as this pine hawkmoth (above), have clever **camouflage** to help them blend in with their backgrounds.*

From caterpillar to adult

When it is fully grown, a caterpillar changes into a pupa, or chrysalis. Inside the pupa, its body changes completely, and it gradually becomes a winged adult.

After several weeks, a pupa (below) splits open and an adult, such as this peacock butterfly, emerges.

If you spot a hairy caterpillar, such as this 'woolly bear' or tiger moth caterpillar, it's best not to touch it. Sometimes the hairs can give you a rash.

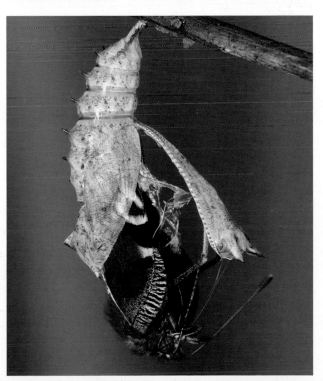

Grasshoppers and crickets

If you go for a walk through a grassy field on a hot summer's day, listen for the buzzing sound of grasshoppers. On warm evenings, you might hear chirping crickets. To spot these insects, you'll need to move very slowly, or they will quickly leap away!

Grasshopper or cricket?

The easiest way to tell grasshoppers and crickets apart is to look at their antennae. A grasshopper has short, stiff antennae. A cricket's antennae are much longer and thinner.

Sounds of the summer

The best time to listen for grasshoppers and crickets is between June and September. This is when the males use their calls to attract females and warn off other males. Crickets make their musical chirping by rubbing their wings together. Grasshoppers rub their legs against their wings.

Hopper habitats

You'll find grasshoppers, such as the meadow grasshopper (below), in almost all parts of Britain. They like dry, sunny places, and live mainly in fields of long grass and in **hedgerows**.

Of the many species of grasshopper living in Britain, the meadow grasshopper is the only one that cannot fly.

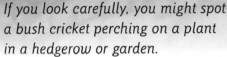

If you look carefully, you might spot a bush cricket perching on a plant in a hedgerow or garden.

The field cricket is one of the rarest insects in Britain.

Blending in

You'll need to look carefully to find grasshoppers and crickets. Most have colouring that blends in with their background. This camouflage makes them very hard to spot!

Long jumpers

Grasshoppers and crickets are well known for their jumping skills. They have long, powerful back legs and can leap great distances when they sense danger.

Superior senses

Grasshoppers and crickets have excellent vision, and will nearly always see you coming! Their eyes can look in many directions at once. They can also detect movements in the air, using small hairs at the end of their bodies.

Rare cricket

Field crickets have never been very common in Britain, but their numbers have dropped in recent years. The good news is that **conservation** efforts are helping them make a comeback. You can find out more about the possible reasons for their decline and what is being done to help them on the Natural England website (see page 2).

Dragonflies and damselflies

Among the most exciting and stunning of all insects you'll find in Britain are dragonflies and damselflies. You'll see them darting through the air on warm summer days.

At home by the water

Dragonflies and damselflies spend most of their time close to water, where they lay their eggs. Look for them near to ponds, rivers, streams, lakes and canals.

Flying ace

One of the first things you'll notice about a dragonfly is its incredible flying skills. It is among the fastest flying insects in the world, reaching speeds of over 35 kph. As it hunts for insects, it can change direction in an instant, fly backwards and even hover like a helicopter.

Wonderful wings

You might wonder what makes a dragonfly such an acrobatic flyer. Unlike most other insects, a dragonfly can flap its two sets of wings separately. This gives it very good control when it's flying.

Amazing eyes

If you're lucky, you might see a dragonfly resting. Look carefully at its huge eyes, which almost cover its head.

This is a southern hawker dragonfly. You might see one flying over slow-flowing water, but they can often be seen in gardens, too.

Hungry young

Dragonflies and damselflies spend most of their lives underwater, as larvae called nymphs. They are fierce hunters, using their powerful jaws to feed on small fish and insects. A good way to find dragonfly and damselfly nymphs is to go pond dipping (see page 30).

The transformers

When a dragonfly or damselfly nymph is fully grown, it goes through an extraordinary change. First, it climbs up a plant stem. Then, its body splits open at the back. Soon, an adult dragonfly or damselfly crawls out and takes to the air.

Dragonfly nymphs live underwater for between two months and three years.

Dragon or damsel?

Damselflies and dragonflies look quite similar, so how can you tell them apart? Damselflies have thinner bodies and smaller eyes. When they are at rest, damselflies hold their wings together above their bodies, while dragonflies keep their wings stretched out.

Eye

Dragonflies, such as this four-spotted chaser, have excellent vision and the biggest eyes in the insect world!

Like all damselflies, this blue demoiselle has eyes that are wide apart, on either side of its head.

Bugs

We often use the term 'bug' to describe all kinds of insects, spiders and other creepy-crawlies, but true bugs are a very special kind of insect. You'll find them in many different habitats, and there might even be some bugs a little too close to home!

What is a bug?

There are about 2,000 different species of bug in Britain, but they all have one thing in common. They have unusual tube-like, piercing mouthparts that can suck liquids, such as sap from plants.

Walking on water

If there's a pond in your local area, look out for some fast-moving bugs on the surface. These are pond skaters. They have special front legs to catch insects that fall in the water.

You can find pond skaters almost anywhere where there is fresh water.

Shield bugs

You will find shield bugs on leaves in gardens, parks and woodlands. If you disturb one, you'll find out why they are also known as stink bugs. They produce a horrible smelling liquid when they sense danger.

You can recognise a shield bug, such as this forest bug, by its shield-shaped body.

Of all the world's insects, aphids are among the most destructive to plants.

Aphid attack

Summer is the time to look for aphids on garden plants. You'll find green ones, black ones and pink ones and they won't disappear when you approach! These bugs cause a huge amount of damage to plants, as they suck sap from their stems, leaves and buds.

Blood suckers

Most bugs suck sap from plants, but bedbugs only drink blood. At night, these tiny brown bugs crawl out of their hiding places and use their piercing mouthparts to suck blood from animals, including sleeping humans!

Cuckoo spit

If you see a blob of frothy liquid on the stem of a plant, look carefully and you might see a bug larva inside. We often call this frothy foam cuckoo spit, but in fact it's made by the larvae of bugs called froghoppers.

The froth we call cuckoo spit protects froghopper larvae from predators and stops them from drying out.

Beetles

No matter where you live in Britain, you won't have to look far to find a beetle. Beetles are the most varied of all insects, with around 400,000 species worldwide. Get down on your hands and knees and see how many kinds you can discover.

On the ground

One of the first beetles you are likely to come across is a ground beetle. These are predators with powerful jaws.

Heavy armour

When you see a beetle scuttling about, you might wonder where its wings are. The armour it seems to be wearing is in fact its front pair of wings. These wings, called the elytra, form a hard, protective cover for the delicate flight wings underneath.

Most ground beetles are black or brown but some, such as this fierce, fast-moving green tiger beetle, are more brightly coloured.

When a beetle takes to the air (above), its elytra open up so it can use its flight wings underneath.

A grub's life

Look under a pile of rotting wood and you might see some beetle grubs, or larvae. Beetle larvae sometimes live for a year or more before changing into pupae. When they emerge as adults, they may only live for a few weeks – just long enough to breed.

Beetle food

Many beetles feed on minibeasts such as worms, spiders and ants. Others feast on leaves, stems and roots. But you might be surprised by some beetles' food choices. The larvae of carpet beetles munch on woollen rugs, and the only thing on the dung beetle's menu is smelly animal poo!

This stag beetle larva will live for up to six years feeding on rotten wood.

Welcome to the garden!

You'll easily recognise the spotty ladybird. This is the gardener's favourite beetle. Ladybirds have enormous appetites for tiny aphids and other garden **pests** that can damage plants.

A ladybird can eat up to 5,000 aphids in its lifetime.

Worms

Everyone is familiar with wiggly worms. They may seem quite ordinary, but of all the minibeasts in our neighbourhoods, the worm is one of the most important – and one of the easiest to find!

Bristly burrowers

With no eyes, ears, legs or bones, an earthworm's body is perfect for burrowing in soil. It is made up of lots of ring-like parts, or segments, which are covered in tiny bristles. These help the worm to move and grip the sides of its tunnels.

Earthy diet

You might wonder what an earthworm finds to eat as it burrows into the soil. The answer is simple – it eats the soil! The leftovers pass out of the worm's body and form squiggly piles called casts (below).

Nature's recyclers

Earthworms have an important part to play in nature. As they tunnel beneath our feet, they mix up **nutrients** in the soil. This keeps the soil healthy and helps plants to grow.

Finding worms

The easiest way to find earthworms is to dig a hole in the ground. Search through the soil you have dug out. You will be surprised how many you find.

Woodlice

You're sure to have lots of woodlice hiding in your neighbourhood. With their armoured bodies and 14 legs, these minibeasts are unlike any others you'll find.

Hiding places

Woodlice love damp, dark places, where they feed on rotting wood and plants. Look for them scuttling about in cellars, under plant pots and stones, and in piles of logs.

Shell suits

It might look as though woodlice are wearing suits of armour. This armour is a woodlouse's hard outer shell, or exoskeleton, which protects its soft body underneath.

Up close

If you find some woodlice, gently scoop a few up and put them in a tray or shallow container, so you can have a closer look. You might be able to see their antennae. They use these to feel their way around.

If you disturb a woodlouse, it might protect itself by curling up.

Crusty cousins

Woodlice belong to a group of animals called crustaceans, which also includes crabs and lobsters.

Curling up

A woodlouse's shell is made up of lots of overlapping sections. These help the woodlouse to bend. Woodlice sometimes curl up into tiny balls when they feel threatened.

Antennae

Spiders

Like it or not, you'll find it easy to spot a spider! You might see one stuck in your bath or scuttling across your bedroom floor. They might not be your favourite minibeasts, but spiders are among the most fascinating you'll find.

Amazing arachnids

Spiders are not insects, but belong to a group of animals called arachnids. Like all arachnids, spiders have eight legs, and their bodies are made up of two parts. Almost all spiders are **carnivores**, feeding on insects and other minibeasts.

House guest

You're most likely to see large, brown house spiders in the autumn, when the males come out of their hiding places to find a mate. They sometimes fall into baths by accident and cannot escape. You can also find them in sheds and piles of wood.

Spider stats

- Spiders have existed on Earth for about 350 million years.
- There are around 40,000 known species of spider in the world.
- In Britain, we have around 700 different species of spider.

There is no need to be frightened of house spiders. They will not hurt you.

Wonderful webs

A good time to see garden spiders is in the early morning, especially in the autumn. If you're lucky, you will see some beautiful webs, sparkling with **dew** or frost. Garden spiders weave webs between plant stems to catch their prey. Once the web is made, the spider hides and waits.

Insect traps

Garden spiders remain attached to their webs by a single thread of silk. Using this they can detect even the slightest movement in their web. When an insect gets caught, the spider scurries over and injects poison into its prey.

Liquid diet

When the spider is ready for its meal, it first releases juice from its stomach on to the body of its victim. This juice turns its prey into liquid, which the spider then sucks up.

This garden spider has caught a hoverfly in its web.

Spider silk

Spiders make their webs from strong, fine silk, which they produce using special body parts called spinnerets. There are around 30 m of silk in each web that a garden spider makes and the silk is stronger than steel of the same weight.

Centipedes and millipedes

If you lift up a stone in a shady corner, you might see some minibeasts with lots of legs. Centipedes and millipedes seem quite similar, but they are more different than you might think – and it's not just in the number of legs!

Carnivorous critters

Like most centipedes, this common brown centipede (below) is a fast-moving carnivore. It scurries around at night on its 30 legs, feeding on insects, slugs and spiders. Centipedes have special claws on the side of their heads to inject poison into their prey.

At home in the dark

During the day, you'll find centipedes in damp, dark places. If you disturb one, it will scurry away quickly to hide from the light.

Marvellous myriapods

Centipedes and millipedes belong to a group of minibeasts called myriapods, which means 'lots of legs'. If you look carefully, you'll see their bodies are made up of many different segments.

Common brown centipedes are reddish brown, with one pair of legs on each body segment.

Hundreds and thousands

The name centipede means 'a hundred feet', and millipede means 'a thousand feet', but not all millipedes have more legs than centipedes. Most centipedes have between 30 and 350 legs and millipedes have between 36 and 400 legs.

Millipede menu

Unlike centipedes, millipedes are vegetarians. They feed mainly on rotting plants, but sometimes eat young shoots and leaves.

Ancient animals

Millipedes were the first creatures to breathe air and live on land. Before then, all the world's creatures lived in the sea.

Slow but safe

Millipedes move more slowly than centipedes, so they can't easily run for cover when they sense danger. If you disturb one, it will defend itself by curling up into a coil.

A millipede curls up to protect its legs and the soft underside of its body.

You can recognise a black millipede by its shiny black body and white legs.

Snails and slugs

Wherever your neighbourhood is, it won't have a shortage of slugs and snails! These munching minibeasts come out at night to nibble on leafy plants. You'll know where they've been from their silvery trails of slime.

Garden gourmets

One of the best places to look for slugs and snails is in a garden. Gardens provide plenty of tasty plants for them to eat and lots of safe places to shelter.

Shell security

All snails have hard shells to protect their soft bodies. When it is resting, a snail pulls its body inside its shell. This stops its body from drying out and protects it from predators.

No rush!

Most garden snails move at around 1 m per hour. It's not very fast, but there's no hurry. At that pace, they can explore much of an average British garden in one night.

One of the snails you are most likely to see is the common garden snail.

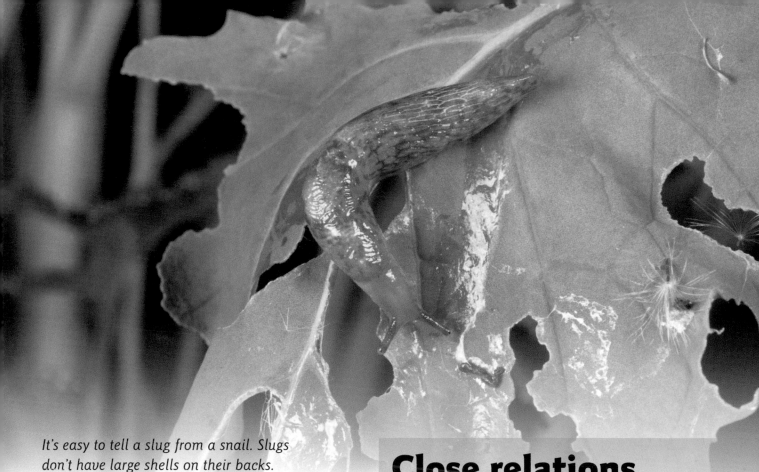

It's easy to tell a slug from a snail. Slugs don't have large shells on their backs.

Damp days

Slugs and snails are most active at night or just after rain. In the daytime, they usually find damp places to rest. Look for them under stones, under flowerpots and in piles of logs.

Sliding along

As they creep along on their soft body, or 'foot', slugs and snails release slimy mucus. This helps them glide easily and protects the underside of their body.

In the water

If there is a pond or slow-moving river in your neighbourhood, it is sure to be home to some snails. Freshwater snails live on **algae** and decaying matter at the bottom of the water.

Of the 50 species of freshwater snails living in Britain, the great pond snail is the largest.

Close relations

Snails and slugs make up a group of animals called gastropods, which means 'stomach foot'. Gastropods are a type of mollusc. Most molluscs, such as octopuses and squid, live in the sea.

Watching minibeasts

It's fun to take a close look at insects and minibeasts so you can learn more about their bodies and how they behave.

Here are some things you might need:
- Yoghurt pots, jars or clear plastic containers to put minibeasts in.
- A net and plastic container for pond dipping.
- A torch for seeing minibeasts at night.
- A magnifying glass.
- A **field guide** to help you identify the minibeasts you find.
- Some minibeasts!

Safety first ⚠

For safety, always have an adult with you when you go pond dipping. Be especially careful around the edge of the pond and stay out of the water.

Tree shake

A simple way to find lots of minibeasts is to lay an old white sheet or pillow case under a tree and give the branches a firm shake. You will be surprised how many different species fall out of the tree.

Telltale signs

You can tell where some minibeasts have been from the clues they leave behind. Slugs and snails leave trails of slime, caterpillars leave holes in leaves and worms leave casts on the surface of soil or sand.

Up close

If you want to look at the minibeasts you find more closely, you can look at them through a magnifying glass. Always handle minibeasts gently and put them back as soon as you have finished looking at them.

Pond dipping is a good way to find a huge variety of minibeasts. Gently sweep a net through the water and empty it into a container.

A magnifying glass will help you take a close look at the minibeasts you find.

Classification of minibeasts

To understand plants and animals, scientists look at their similarities and differences and sort them into groups. This is called classification.

Grouping plants and animals

Plants are divided into flowering plants and non-flowering plants. Animals are divided into those with backbones (vertebrates) and those without backbones (minibeasts, or invertebrates).

Grouping invertebrates

Invertebrates are divided into different groups (called phyla). These groups include worms, arthropods (animals with jointed legs), molluscs (snails and slugs) and other kinds of minibeast.

Invertebrates

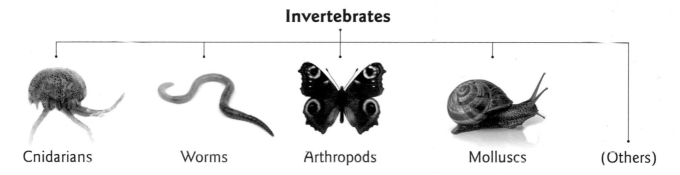

| Cnidarians | Worms | Arthropods | Molluscs | (Others) |

From phylum to species

Each phylum of invertebrate is divided into smaller groups called classes. Insects are one of the classes of animal that belong within the group called arthropods.

Arthropods

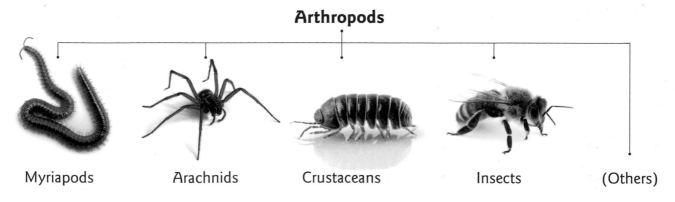

| Myriapods | Arachnids | Crustaceans | Insects | (Others) |

Classes are further divided into orders, then into families and genera. Species are the smallest groups – they are types of minibeasts that are so similar that they can breed together.

Glossary

abdomen the back part of the body of an insect or spider

algae simple, non-flowering plants without true roots, stems and leaves

antennae feelers on the head of an insect or other minibeast

bacteria tiny living things that can cause disease

camouflage a way of making things blend into the background

carnivores animals that eat meat

conservation protecting and preserving natural environments and living things

dew tiny drops of water formed at night

field guide a book used for identification

habitat a place where animals or plants live

hedgerows rows of trees or bushes

invertebrates animals that do not have backbones

larvae insects in the stage of their development between egg and pupa

mouthparts the parts of the mouth of an insect or other minibeast

nectar a sweet liquid produced by flowers

nutrients substances that are needed to keep animals and plants alive

order a rank of living things made up of families that share similar characteristics

pests animals that damage plants

pollen a fine yellow powder made by flowers

pollinate to put pollen into a flower so it develops fruit and seeds

predators animals that kill and eat other animals

prey an animal that is hunted by another animal for food

pupae insects in the stage of their development between larvae and adults

queen bee a female bee that can produce eggs

species a type of animal or plant that breeds with others of the same kind

thorax the part of an insect's body between its head and abdomen

Index